Rahab: Beyond Risqué

RAHAB
Beyond Risqué

Rahab: Beyond Risqué

RAHAB
BEYOND RISQUÉ

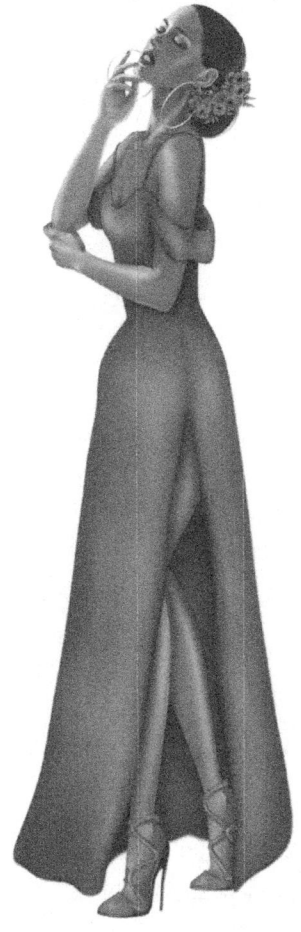

A Historical Fiction
by
Dr. Chioma

Faithful Series

Copyright © 2024 Dr. Chioma

All rights reserved.

ISBN: 9798327989634
Imprint: Independently published

To my parents.

Rahab: Beyond Risqué

"I will show mercy to anyone I choose, and

I will show compassion to anyone I choose."

'It is God who decides to show mercy. We can neither choose it nor work for it. In the Scriptures, God told Pharaoh, "I have appointed you for the very purpose of displaying My power in you and to spread My fame throughout the earth." So, you see, God chooses to show mercy to some, and He chooses to harden the hearts of others, so they refuse to listen. Well then, you might say, "Why does God blame people for not responding? Haven't they simply done what He makes them do?"'

'No, don't say that. Who are you, a mere human being, to argue with God? Should the thing that was created say to the One who created it, "Why have You made me like this?" When a Potter makes jars out of clay, doesn't He have a right to use the same lump of clay to make one jar for decoration and another to throw garbage into? In the same way, God has the right to show His anger and power. He is very patient with those on whom His anger falls, who are destined for destruction. He does this to make the riches of His glory shine even brighter on those to whom He shows mercy, who were prepared in advance for glory. And we are among those whom He selected, both from the Jews and from the Gentiles.'

'Concerning the Gentiles (i.e. the non-Jews), God said the following:

"Those who were not My people, I will now call My people. And I will love those whom I did not love before." "Then, at the place where they were told, 'You are not My

people,' there they will be called 'children of the living God.'"
Romans 9: 15 - 26 (NLT).

"Then I will sow her (i.e. Israel) for Myself in the earth, And I will have mercy on her who had not obtained mercy; Then I will say to those who were not My people, 'You are My people!' And they shall say, You are my God'".
Hosea 2: 23 (NKJV).

"Let us therefore come boldly to the throne of grace, that we may obtain mercy and find grace to help in time of need."
Hebrews 4: 16 (NKJV).

Author's Note

Born and raised with very limited exposure to the pure, unadulterated Word of God, I struggled to understand how historical Bible stories were applicable to the world around me. As I grew older and read the Bible for myself, I began to develop a clearer understanding of the Bible as being alive and relevant to my world today.

> *"For the word of God is living and powerful, and sharper than any two-edged sword, piercing even to the division of soul and spirit, and of joints and marrow, and is a discerner of the thoughts and intents of the heart.*
> **- Hebrews 4: 12 (NKJV).**

Prologue

This historical fiction attempts to retell the Bible story of Rahab from a relatable setting and context. It is the first of the Faithful Series, which retell Bible-based historical truths from today's point of view without compromising the essence of God's Word— faith, repentance, and salvation.

Rahab the harlot played a significant role in bringing down the walls of Jericho. When Joshua sent two men to spy on the land of Jericho, she hid these men and protected them from the king who sought to capture them. Although a harlot, Rahab acted out of faith and begged both men to save her family when they returned to destroy the land of Jericho. Clearly, God can show His divine mercy to anyone, and harlots are not exempt!

In this fictional version, Rahab is a harlot in modern day New York City. She played a significant role in hiding two men of God on a revival mission in the city of New York. Despite her risqué lifestyle as a harlot, Rahab acted out of faith to protect these men on their mission. Find out how God in turn showed Rahab and her family mercy.

Rahab: Beyond Risqué

CONTENTS

Acknowledgments   xxi

1   A Risqué Appointment   1

2   A Divine Appointment   Pg 5

3   Surprise Visitors   Pg 17

4   Family Time   Pg 29

5   A Declaration of Faith   Pg 33

6   Revival and Repentance   Pg 41

7   Delayed but Not Denied   Pg 49

8   Deliverance and Destruction   Pg 57

Epilogue   Pg 63

About the Author   Pg 67

Acknowledgments

I thank God for blessing me with such a loving family.

In every season, they have soldiered with me. To my husband Ted, we are in this together. To my children, Faith, and Emmanuel, you continue to make me a better person. I love you all.

Modupe Olatunji, thank you for your professionalism and candor. With love, you edited this work, and I can't thank you enough for your gift of time.

Dele Nonye-John, your patience to see this work become complete will never be forgotten. Thank you for carefully recording and editing the audio version of this work. You understood the assignment, and for that, I am grateful.

CHAPTER 1
A Risqué Appointment

The 11am Sunday morning service had just concluded when Rahab heard a whisper from behind: "How about 9pm tonight?" She turned to find Larry behind her. Unsurprised, she whispered back, "Show some respect for the house of the Lord."

"What do you mean?" Larry asked with a mischievous smile. "With that gorgeous dress on you, I managed to wait for the service to finish. That's respectful enough!"

Rahab rolled her eyes and began to walk away in her usual seductive gait. Larry followed her and continued speaking to her when she sharply replied, "Leave me alone. You take up my time for nothing." She always knew how to threaten his confidence and make him want to prove a point to her very own financial advantage.

This wasn't the first time he had heard her say such a thing. It's a trap he has come to expect and enjoy. "You didn't say that the last time you swiped my American Express on that little gadget of yours. Besides, I know how to make you feel very good, you know."

"Really?" She paused to look him straight in the eye and added, "I just make you think so, but it's really not so. Besides, I deserve it after several years of keeping your lustful secrets." She winked at him deviously and began to walk away again, but he didn't stop following her. As soon as Rahab had walked far enough from the view of other church members, she stopped and stretched out her palm at Larry.

"Well, if you must see me tonight, you have to confirm your appointment in advance."

"Is that how to treat a loyal friend?" Larry asked.

"Loyal Indeed," Rahab says.

Reluctantly, he dipped his hand into his pocket and brought out his American Express Platinum card from his wallet. Before he could hand it to her, she snatched it out of his hand, and pulled out the credit card reader to swipe the Amex card for the usual amount; then, she proceeded to select the 25% option for tips. She returns the hard metal card and presents him with her phone screen to sign away.

"See you at 7pm tonight." She said as she approached her brand-new Mercedes coupe.

"No, I asked to come at 9pm."

"Too bad! I'm expecting guests at that time. See you at 7pm or forget about it, Larry."

Reluctantly, he agreed to meet at 7pm and began to walk away with a lustful smile on his wrinkled face.

CHAPTER 2
A Divine Appointment

Rahab had been in the bathtub for a while and lost track of time when her phone began to ring. She had ignored several text message alerts to relax for a moment. She looked at the time and it was already 9:15pm. It must be her guests, she thought to herself and hurried out of the bathtub to answer the call.

"Hello?"

"Hello, my name is Kofi and I'm here with my brother in the Lord, Chidi. We want to confirm if the Air B and B reservation for tonight is still available."

"Absolutely." She responded.

"Great! We just left the airport and we're in the Uber ride on our way to you. The ETA shows we're about 25 minutes away."

"Alright, see you when you get here." She said and hung up.

Quickly, she called the front desk lady, Candice, to inform her that she was expecting two guests, Kofi and Chidi.

Candice began her usual speech: "I hope you know that renting out your Penthouse..."

"Is against the Homeowners Covenant Agreement." Rahab joined Candice to finish the sentence and continued to add: "Candice, I know all that. For the records, I'm not renting it out. Thanks for the reminder. I'll see you in the morning. Have a nice day."

That was code for, 'I know you know what I'm doing, but I'll tip you for looking past the HOA rules.'

Rahab owns two apartments in a luxurious New York building. She lives in the penthouse on the top floor, while her parents and two of her brothers live in the other apartment, two floors beneath hers. She's street-smart and business minded. Sometimes, she rents out her guest room to tourists and visitors from out of town. Her listing on Air B and B has allowed her to easily make a passive income; occasionally, she finds new clients for her adult services from her accommodation side hustle. Thankfully, nobody from the HOA has found out yet because she had found crafty ways of avoiding detection. So far, it has been working for her.

Renting out her guest room helped her save up a down payment to buy an extra apartment in the same building for her family. This allowed Rahab to keep her family close by while providing for them. Her father was a Vietnam war veteran suffering severe PTSD as a former prisoner of war in Vietnam. He was beaten blind while in captivity. Her mother was the primary caregiver to her father. Rahab's mom suffered depression and for a long time, she had not seen her parents put on a smile.

The emotional and financial pressure to care for her family was always on Rahab. Her parents were both in therapy but made little progress. Now, in their late sixties, they could use a miracle. No matter how difficult the circumstances were with her parents, she always remained positive and hopeful. Her strength was helpful to them, and she had to stay strong.

It was almost time for Kofi and Chidi to arrive. She remembered Larry was watching Fox News on her living room couch. He knows what she does for a living and doesn't care as long as she makes time for him and keeps their affairs confidential. Larry has been divorced twice and is now single. They had known each other for over a decade; even while he was married, he was her regular client.

Larry is not your average client; he's clingy and has low self-esteem. He showers her with money and expensive gifts. Sometimes, she accompanies him on business trips out of the country. However, they fly separate flights and avoid being seen together because Larry is a multi-millionaire banking executive. He knows how to live an ordinary life without flaunting his wealth or personal affairs. Therefore, very few people have any idea of his net worth, and Rahab is unofficially among the few. She knows how to intimately boost his confidence. For him, Rahab has become an addiction he's not willing to give up.

Larry is a regular client that she treasures; giving him small doses of this truth always seems to be the validation that Larry needs to boost his self-esteem regularly. It keeps him wanting to please her financially, while she also pleases him in return. He is just a pleaser when it comes to Rahab. She understands his need for constant validation and that makes him feel so good. Rahab is an expert at belittling him as bait for him to try to prove a financial point. She knows how to make him feel good about himself as soon as he is paid up. They have a weird dynamic, which they have both managed to sustain for more than a decade and counting.

She got out of the bathtub, rinsed off the soap, and began to get dressed. She picked out a red dress that was long all the way to her ankles. The slit ran all the way up from her ankles to her buttocks. Rahab put on some makeup with red lipstick to match her dress. She wasn't done with the color matching. She selected a pair of red high-heeled sandals to match all the red. The only thing that was not red was her gold hoop earrings. To finalize her look, she pulled her hair back in a bun and sealed it with a hair clip that was covered with a design of red roses.

Rahab knows how to look the part for her lifestyle, but she always does it with class. That's how she attracts a high-profile clientele. They are mostly CEOs, celebrities, high-profile religious men, etc. They are usually people who have something to lose, so they pay her well for exclusivity and confidentiality.

She quickly mixed herself a light cocktail to numb her mind for the unpredictability of her evening. She had barely taken a sip when her doorbell rang. She went to her living room and told Larry it was time to leave if he didn't want her rental guests to see him. He lazily grabbed the keys to his two-seater Porsche and began to leave through the other exit.

Rahab took another sip and quickly dropped the cocktail glass on her coffee table, freshened her breath with chewing gum, sprayed some perfume, dimmed the lights, and straightened her dress. Hips swinging, she made for the door.

As a safety routine, she looked through the peephole to confirm it was Kofi and Chidi. She had to be staring at them from the peephole. Confirming to herself that her guests had arrived, she opened the door and greeted both men politely.

The names on the booking seemed foreign, though she hadn't paid much attention. But one look at Kofi and Chidi, she knew they had to be Africans fresh out of the continent. They wore traditional African attire, and their motherland-themed hand luggage did not fit into the New York fashion and travel atmosphere.

Both men began to speak at the same time and quickly held back as a show of courtesy to each other. While they briefly waited out the awkward moment, Rahab took in their thick African accent. Clearly, these men had come from the motherland with only a hand luggage each. Chidi broke the ice and apologetically stepped into the apartment and beckoned Kofi to follow. As soon as they were in the apartment, Kofi begged her to shut the door for their safety.

"Don't worry," she begins, "this is a safe building, and the crime rate is almost nonexistent around here. Safety is why you're paying so much, you know." At this point, Rahab switched on her bright lights to take a good look at the men while they also glanced around every corner of her luxurious apartment.

"Well then", she says, "may I have your identification to confirm who you really are?" They said "yes," and both produced a green passport with ECOWAS boldly written on it.

"ECOWAS? "What country is that?"

"It's not a country; it's a group of countries," replied Chidi. "Our respective countries are listed right next to the ECOWAS logo on our passports. It stands for Economic Community of West African States. We are both West Africans from different countries - Nigeria and Ghana. However, we are one, just like Canada is part of North America."

"Our countries not only have a lot in common, but they have also come together to establish common economic interests within the region and beyond," added Kofi.

"That's interesting. Are you here for business, then?"

They both responded at the same time. Chidi said yes, while Kofi said no. "Well, sort of," begins Chidi. "We have been sent to America by our lead pastor, Apostle Joshua Nun. We are on a revival mission to make disciples and baptize them in the name of the Father, the Son - Jesus Christ and His Holy Spirit. That is the business we have been divinely assigned to carry out in several parts of America."

Kofi added that this type of business is not for money, which is why he responded "no" to her question. "We are not in town for financial business, so to speak."

"He's correct," Chidi continued. "We're not here for financial reasons, but our work will bring freedom, including financial freedom: 'For who the Son sets free is free indeed!' " exclaimed Chidi. "For the Spirit of the Lord is upon us. He has sent us to preach the gospel to the poor; He has sent us to heal the brokenhearted, to proclaim liberty to the captives, including financial captives. And recovery of sight to the blind. To set at liberty to those who are oppressed; To proclaim the acceptable year of the Lord."

"Hmm, did I hear you say the blind? Did you really say the blind?" Rahab questioned him.

"Yes, it's a scripture that I can share with you. Let me quickly look it up." Almost immediately, he pulls out the scripture from the Bible app on his phone and joyfully points out Luke chapter four verse 18 to Rahab.

"Here," he went on, "you should also take a look at our ministry on social media and get a glimpse of what we are talking about." Rahab watched him scroll through the pages of different social media accounts. From what she saw, they were healing the sick, the crippled, and the blind. They were praying over the oppressed and carrying out multiple deliverance services with miracles that seemed too good to be true. She was moved by what she saw and had goose bumps all over her arms. She had many thoughts and was yet to articulate them when Kofi interrupted the moment.

"May I please use the toilet?"

"You mean the restroom? Sure." As Rahab began to direct them towards the guest room bathroom, she heard the back exit door slam gently. She realized that it must have been Larry who was just leaving. She apologized that a friend had just exited from the back door. Kofi admitted to seeing a man's back rushing away while they spoke. He assumed it was someone who lived with her.

Rahab pointed out the door to the guest room and instructed Kofi to use the attached guest bathroom. She had been holding their passports in her hand. At this time, she handed both passports back to Chidi and thought it would be best to continue the conversation later. She would later go back to their social media handles to comb through posts of their revival ministry for herself.

Rahab went to her bedroom, picked up her purse and locked her safe. She adjusted her sandal straps and was ready to leave for her next appointment with another client. One last look in the mirror to validate her beauty, she was ready to be on her way.

She was running late and made a call to apologize to the client. He nagged and yelled at her a lot as if he was in "Hell's Kitchen TV" show. It never bothered her as long as she was paid, which he knew just how to do.

She offered to cancel, but he refused and demanded extra time for her delay. She accepted and kept it moving. This client was the CEO of a major cosmetic company in America. He had a fetish for things unimaginable and Rahab knew how to play along.

"Are you going out?" she heard the familiar African accent behind her.

"Yes." She responded.

"In that dress? I thought it was your sleepwear."

"Haba, Kofi! It's not your place to ask her that," Chidi intervened and apologized for Kofi's unintended rudeness.

It's difficult to offend Rahab. Her line of business has taught her to overlook offenses, especially from men. She simply winked at them and said, "See you later, guys!" And she was out the door.

CHAPTER 3
Surprise Visitors

It was around 6am when Rahab drove into the parking garage. She went straight into her apartment and began to undress. Before she could slip into something comfortable, the landline rang. The only people who called her landline were telemarketers and the front desk staff. One of her favorite perks about living here was the security protocol. She answered and heard the morning shift staff inform her that she had guests. Surprised, she asked them to identify themselves.

They said they were Pastors Derrick and Richard from her church. They had never visited her, so she simply assumed they knew her guests and came by to plan the revival mission together.

"Please let them upstairs," she says. As soon as she hung up, she threw on a rather short robe and assumed all she had to do was let them in to see Chidi and Kofi while she took a shower and caught some sleep. She had barely made her way to the front door when she heard a loud, persistent knock on the front door.

"I'll be right there," she yelled as she made her way to the door.

As her usual safety habit, she looked through the peephole to find both men standing at the door with a rather unfriendly demeanor. They were the assistant pastors to the senior pastor at her church. Before she had time to wonder why they had to come so early, she noticed Pastor Derrick pull out a gun and quickly put it back in his jacket after Pastor Richard gave him a sign to hide it. For a moment, she doubted what she saw and began to shrug it off when one of them yelled out, "Kunta Kinte, open the damn door!"

Shocked by what she had just heard from these so-called sastors, she considered ignoring them but felt it was too late because they had already heard her when she yelled, "I'll be right there."

Contrary to what she had assumed, Pastors Derrick and Richard may not be friends of her guests from Africa. She immediately suspected they were in conflict and she became very cautious. What could Kofi and Chidi have done to them? And how did they know they were at her place? They are just Christians from Africa, and they showed me their social media ministry, she recalled.

Thanks to her quick thinking, Rahab put up her door chain and unlocked the door. She looked them in the face and asked why they had come so early. Richard demanded that she open the door if she didn't want any trouble.

Without feeling any embarrassment, she showed them a glimpse of her short-length robe and told them she'll be back to open the door as soon as she could get properly dressed.

Given Rahab's line of business, Richard smirked and told her it wasn't necessary.

"Only if you were paying me. By the way, I don't care about your business. I need a few minutes to get decent for your unannounced visit; you can wait or leave."

Rahab quickly locked the door behind her and rushed into the guest room to wake Chidi and Kofi. Confirming her suspicion, they were not expecting anyone to visit them at Rahab's apartment. Their visit was a very short one; besides, they didn't have any friends or family in New York. They were in town to privately explore prospects of a revival and deliverance event that would win souls for the Lord. Period. They begged her not to give them in, especially if Derrick and Richard seemed armed.

Rahab quickly glanced around the guest room and noticed they had barely unpacked their hand luggage. They must have gone straight to bed, she thought. She rushed to grab both hand luggage and hid them in the cupboard under the guest bathroom sink as she told them they had to leave for their own safety. In case they forcefully searched her apartment, she did not want to leave any clue that would suggest Chidi and Kofi were still lodging with her.

Without wasting time, she took them to the rooftop of her penthouse and pointed to the wall that separated her apartment from the other apartment beside hers. Between both walls was a carefully secluded space. Nobody ever notices that space unless you are very familiar with the layout of the penthouse rooftop. Before she rushed back inside, Chidi pulled her back, laid his right hand on her forehead, and said to her, "We cover you with the blood of Jesus."

Unsure about how to respond, she thanked them and hurriedly began to make her way back into the apartment.

It had been about a couple of minutes, which felt like forever. Rahab headed to her own bedroom and threw on a pair of denim shorts and a T-shirt. They began knocking again, and it was so unrelenting that she could hear it while she was still away from her front door. She remembered to lock off her balcony doors that led to the rooftop and rushed back to get the front door.

Rahab opened the front door slightly to maintain a safe distance. One of the men grabbed the doorknob and opened it wide as they shoved past her. Everything about their visit spelt evil. They demanded to see the guests at her house.

"We want to see the Africans who came to you." As Pastor Richard was still speaking, a third man walked in. He was rather casually dressed in an impeccable golf outfit. Away from the diabolic duo, he was just an average-looking man in golf attire. He didn't look as evil as the other two men, but she sensed he was just as evil, if not worse. She watched him steal lecherous glances at her legs before he shoved her to her impeccable white leather sofa and gave Rahab a dead look.

Of course, she recognized him. This is the senior pastor at her church. This is the man in charge of everything, she thought to herself. He is the lead pastor of the mega church she attends every Sunday. She had no idea why he was in her apartment or what he had against Chidi and Kofi. What on earth are they all doing in her apartment? And how did the third man make it past the front desk?

He deliberately put his hand on her shoulder to threaten her personal space. Maintaining the cold stare, he demanded to see the African Revivalists.

"They are not here. I asked them to leave," she lied, not knowing why she felt a pressing need to protect Kofi and Chidi from these familiar but evil-looking men. They glanced around the luxurious apartment as if hoping to spot the men. They noticed the almost full cocktail glass with lipstick stain sitting on her coffee table. She had forgotten to remove it yesterday and its isolated presence seemed to convince these evil men that she was by herself.

Somewhat convinced, they decided to take a look for themselves as they made their way around the 1,500-square-foot apartment. When one of them made it to the balcony door, he noticed it was locked and began to unlock it when the boss called them back and turned the attention back to Rahab.

"Where did they go?" He asked her. "If you don't want any trouble, tell us where the African Revivalists went."

Rahab found herself saying a silent prayer before she began to speak. "Indeed, the strangers came here, but I sent them away when I found out they were Revivalists." I'm expecting some high-profile clients who made last-minute appointments. I didn't want anyone preaching to me about my lifestyle or the way I like to dress. Besides, there won't be any space for my clients, who are more important to me.

But I do remember they said something about making a Hilton reservation with their membership points. Hurry up and check nearby Hilton hotels before it is too late."

The three men glanced at one another and began to rush out the door as the senior pastor punched in some numbers on his cell phone to make calls with a sense of urgency.

The whole encounter lasted about 10 minutes, but it felt like ten hours. As soon as she was able to pull herself together, she went to lock the door behind her and headed to the rooftop; delighted they were all safe.

She calls out for Kofi and Chidi in a hushed voice. They went back into the house and she told them the threatening men were pastors from the church she attended. Surprised about this, Kofi and Chidi asked her to tell them more about her church.

"Well, it's a mega church that believes only men should teach, which I think is a form of misogyny in the church. They teach against speaking in tongues. They permit gay marriages, and they teach that God only speaks to them. A lot of their beliefs don't make any sense because they make God seem partial, unfair and mean-spirited. Last month, the church collected offerings to purchase a private jet for the senior pastor. The way we are asked to give and keep giving to the so-called house of God makes our God look very poor and wretched."

Rahab just continued to pour out her heart about the things that did not make sense to her. When she was finished expressing these hypocrisies, she asked Chidi, "But who am I to judge the church when I'm also a sinner with a shameful lifestyle?" She leaned forward to make a plea and said to them: "I know in my heart that the pastors in my church do not have the love of God. They make God look poor and unforgiving. I know God made everything and owns everything. I believe there is grace and mercy. I know that marriage between two women or two men cannot be of God and does not align with His plan to multiply and fill the earth. I also know that women are smart and gifted. If they can teach God's children in schools and lead in their careers, God wants women to also lead in the church; unfortunately, the men in my church are afraid of this. But who am I to speak up? I live a promiscuous lifestyle that pays my bills and some of the men in church patronize me. I'm just like them! A hypocrite."

"If I may ask, what is the name of your church?" asked Kofi.

"It's called Everyone's Light Church of God." Rahab responds. "They teach that we all have our light and need to let it shine. Therefore, if your light was gay, let it shine because God is the creator of light, and He must have made you that way."

"Interesting!" said both men, whose similar accents made it difficult to distinguish their thoughts and speech. They seemed very much aligned in their responses, and questioning. Of course, they also seemed convincingly aligned with God.

Without wasting time, she fixed them some breakfast and hurried them up to finish their meal. When they were done with breakfast, she followed them out from the back door. Good thing her car had tinted windows to avoid detection in case anyone was lurking around. She drove them to New Jersey so they can explore more revival opportunities.

As Kofi and Chidi rode with her in silence, Chidi wondered what her church pastors had against them to feel threatened by their presence in New York. He made up his mind to find out and began to google the name of her church without telling them what he was doing. When they arrived in New Jersey, she bid them goodbye and told them to go in peace.

CHAPTER 4
Family Time

Rather than go straight to her own apartment, Rahab went to her parents' apartment to check on them. She was tired, so she considered a phone call, but she thought it was best to see them instead. As she expected, they were not doing well. The atmosphere was quite depressing as they rarely smiled. She wanted more for them but did not know what else to do. She watched a Netflix movie with them while her father just listened.

At the end of the movie, she checked their fridge to ensure it was still stocked with groceries. Unsurprised, they were out of a few items. She clicked her grocery shopping app on her phone to order their necessities before she went back to her own apartment.

Her parents rarely came to see her because she came to visit them daily. Besides, their circumstances made it quite an inconvenience to visit her. Her brothers, who lived with her parents, were always occupied with their jobs and preferred to text or call. It was better like that anyway so they wouldn't discover her lifestyle if they didn't already have their suspicions. Whenever her parents asked her what she did for a living, she would tell them she worked for herself as a real estate agent.

Rahab hated living a lie. She dropped out of college after her second year. Not that she wasn't smart enough to finish her program in Accounting, but she just did not have the patience. She simply lived life her own way and never looked back. It's been almost fifteen years since she dropped out of college, and she is beginning to seriously consider what to do with the next phase of her life. She can't continue like this forever, she thought to herself.

Rahab eventually made it to her bed around 8pm. Thankfully, she had no appointments and needed every rest she could get. It was an early night for her. She was exhausted from the events that unfolded this morning. She was still wondering how anyone knew that Kofi and Chidi had come to her house. Was her Air B and B account hacked? Did someone trail them from the airport? How did the person know it was her apartment they came to? Why did her church pastors care about these men to threaten their lives?

All these thoughts began to flood her mind when suddenly she remembered! Larry! He saw them. But what did he stand to gain by setting them up if he did? Why did he feel the need to mention it to anyone?

Immediately, she began to call him but quickly changed her mind. *What will I tell him? I like what he does for me, and I don't want to say anything that will upset him.* As quickly as the thought occurred to her, she decided it would probably be safer to avoid pursuing it. She was just glad to be safe now that everything seemed over. Feeling a sense of relief, she fell asleep.

CHAPTER 5
A Declaration of Faith

Rahab woke up to a text message from Chidi. They confirmed their departure from New Jersey to explore the Washington D.C and Maryland area for more revival opportunities. They were to depart the U.S one day after they explored the D.C - Maryland area. She felt compelled to call them.

"Hello, Rahab!" Begins Chidi. "How are you doing? I still can't thank you enough for all your kindness. May our Lord and Savior Jesus Christ reward you abundantly."

"Thank you," she gently responded. "So, tell me, how was New Jersey?"

"God is good. There is definitely a need for a revival here. We went to the homeless shelters and elderly homes, met with some foster care children, and visited some hospital chaplains to explore healing opportunities. We also reached out to some Christian schools and a brothel. As we visited some churches, we met their pastors, and they were excited to partner with us. One church volunteered their high school premises and their church campus for the revival ministry when we return."

You could hear the excitement in Chidi's voice as Kofi joined him in the background with some exciting remarks.

"Unfortunately," Rahab begins, "you could not accomplish this in New York. It was all cut short for your safety."

"Not exactly," he continued. "Thanks to technology, we googled and called the places we needed to reach. It was all phone calls." At this point, he changed the subject.

"By the way, Rahab, your church of Everyone's Light came up during our digital exploration of Revival prospects in the New York area."

"Really?" Rahab asked. "Well, I'm not surprised. It's a big church. Lots of power and influence in the New York area."

"It sure is." Says Chidi. "But did you know the founders of the church are not even born-again Christians?"

"What does that mean?" Rahab asked. "I mean, why does it matter?"

"It means a lot, Rahab. You cannot... well, not you specifically, but nobody, I mean, nobody can bring anybody to the Lord if they are not yet in the presence of the Lord. That means the foundation is not firmly established on the Solid Rock of the Church, Who is Jesus Christ. The Word says in the book of Psalms, 'if the foundation is torn, what can the righteous do?' No matter how much you try, knowing God in that place will be very difficult."

"No wonder!" She exclaimed. "I've always felt a disconnect between their teachings and the Bible stories that my mother read to me as a child. But who am I to know the real difference if I've never read the Bible for myself?"

"My sister, Rahab, I implore you to get to know God for yourself and make time to read His Word, the Bible. That is the only way to know when you are being deceived. Simply read the pure, unadulterated Word of the Living God. No book, religion, pastor, preacher, magazine, or publication can replace knowing the pure, unadulterated Word of God for yourself. That is how you begin to form a personal relationship with God. Besides, it strengthens your prayer life to know the Word of God and pray His Word. That is how His divine will, not our will can be done in your life and on earth."

"Besides," he continued, "Mr. Larry Benson is in the church business for his own pocket and nothing more. He and the fake pastors in your church have no interest in your salvation."

"Wait a minute! Did you say, Larry Benson?"

"Yes, a multi-millionaire banking executive who happens to be the owner of the church. He provided 100% percent of the financing for your church. All the so-called pastors work for him."

"How do you know this?" She asked.

"We did a simple entity search on the New York Secretary of State website. He's quite an influential multi-millionaire in corporate America. He's known to be a ruthless business executive who has no interest in God."

It all began to make sense to Rahab. She had a sharp headache suddenly. She wanted to get off the phone but before she did, she had a few things to say.

"It all makes sense now. When I saw the video of you speaking in tongues on your social media page, I felt something, and it was sincere. I watched the testimonies on your social media pages. These are things that I have never experienced in that church, yet it felt divine. I know in my heart that God is backing what you do. This is why the pastors from my church felt threatened enough to hunt you down. The counterfeit is afraid of the original. They don't want to lose credibility or church membership. It does add up now. Listen to me, Chidi, are you still on the line?"

"Yes," he responded.

"I believe in my heart that God loves me, and He wants sinners like me to come to him, but I don't know where to begin. How can I be saved with my family? Please promise me you will not leave me and my family out of the revival, please? We need a revival. My mom, my dad, my entire family. We need this revival. I want to experience with my family the joy of the Lord that I have seen in your social media videos of past revival events."

"Say no more; the Lord has heard your request. For whatever we ask by faith, according to His will, He hears us."

Chidi promised her they would not forget her or her family when they came back to New York for the Revival. He put the phone on speaker and beckoned Kofi to join him in praying for Rahab over the phone.

It was definitely Larry! He overheard them before he left her apartment that evening. So, he felt threatened and asked his stooges to follow up. What a desperate effort to protect his business interests. She was done with him.

CHAPTER 6
Revival and Repentance

The arena was packed full. Parking space would have been a hassle for Rahab if she had not arrived two hours earlier. Thankfully, Rahab was constantly being updated by Kofi and Chidi. She knew it was a highly anticipated Christian event, so she was well-prepared. She had packed sandwiches and healthy beverages for her parents to stay hydrated. She was over-prepared because there were multiple stands for light refreshments. Her brothers Nathan and Jerry joined them for the Revival. It was a whole family affair, and they were happy to be there.

The Revival was finally here. Kofi and Chidi had come back to New York city with their whole Revival team from Africa. Rahab was grateful to have a front-row view of this experience.

It had been about 45 minutes of praise and worship with prayers and scriptural declarations. She had never seen such an energetic environment that glorified Jesus as Lord and Savior. Something about being here felt right and spiritually enriching. In this atmosphere, nothing bothered Rahab. She felt at peace and said a quick prayer of gratitude. She hasn't prayed or worshipped like this before. Her prayers are usually to ask God for something. This time, she was thanking God for everything. Tears began to roll down her eyes. They were tears of gratitude, tears of peace and tears of joy. There was nothing negative about her tears. For the first time in her life, she felt God was with her, in her and for her. She was in awe of this experience.

A man stepped up to the stage and introduced himself as Apostle Joshua Nun. Next to him was another man whom he introduced as Caleb Jephunneh. Both men seemed well-known by the crowd because as soon as they stepped on to the stage, the crowd began cheering and many broke out praying in tongues. This lasted a few minutes while tears continued to roll down Rahab's eyes. She held Nathan and Jerry close and hugged them tight.

"Hallelujah! Let us take a moment to acknowledge the Holy Spirit for what God is about to do in this moment," announced Apostle Joshua. He began to pray and make prophetic declarations over the body of Christ. The more he prayed in the name of Jesus, the more everyone seemed spiritually uplifted.

Rahab's attention was rudely interrupted by a young boy who sat behind her. He was banging his head on the back of her chair and startled her. She noticed he had a helmet to likely offer him some protection during this impulsive behavior to hit his head on a surface. He made sudden, repetitive attempts to continue this disruption before his mom held him back and apologized to Rahab, saying: "I'm sorry, he has severe autism." She smiled and nodded in acceptance of the apology. It felt like the boy's mom was yelling at her, but Rahab realized that was the only way to be heard over the noise in the arena. The boy himself seemed distracted and never made any eye contact to acknowledge the interruption he had caused.

"It's fine." Rahab responded and followed up with a question. "Do you believe that God can deliver him?"

The woman responded very clearly to say, "We are here because we believe. May God's will be done in my son's life."

They both nodded in agreement and continued worshiping. Apostle Joshua began to make prophetic declarations for deliverance. There were screams from multiple angles of the arena. Clearly, people were being delivered of evil spirits and demons. Some rolled on the floor. Others let out fearful screams. It seemed like controlled chaos. Rahab and her family had never experienced this, but they felt confident because they believed God was behind these men of God.

Next, an announcement was made for anyone in a wheelchair to come forward and receive healing.

Miraculously, many came forward, and began to shout out with joy about their immediate healing. Wheelchairs were abandoned as their owners jumped up for joy. Another declaration was made for the deaf to hear and the blind to see. Rahab and her family quickly directed their attention at her dad in anticipation of a healing miracle. She drew him close and whispered to him to open his eyes. He shook his head in fear and uncertainty as tears rolled down his face.

At this moment, her entire family had all eyes on her dad, looking intently to see if they had received a miracle. Unfortunately, her father could not open his eyes. He just cried uncontrollably. Disappointed that their father had not received a miracle, they still believed and began to collectively repeat the scriptural declarations that Apostle Joshua had made.

"By His stripes, we are healed..."

"Who the Son sets free is free indeed..."

"We do not wrestle against flesh and blood, but against principalities and wicked spirits..."

"But the weapons of our warfare are mighty in God for pulling down strongholds and casting down arguments..."

"We can decree a thing and it shall be established for us, so we decree and declare that daddy has regained his vision..."

"We speak to the spirit of oppression to declare that our family is free from the spirit of blindness and wicked spirits of oppression."

"We cast out depression, and we declare that every yoke of the enemy over our household and future generations is broken!"

"As for me and my household, we shall serve the living God of Apostle Joshua."

As they continued these declarations and prayers, Rahab's father felt for her and whispered to her to come closer. He drew her very close and began to pray into her ears.

"My daughter, Rahab, I declare that you are free from lustful men because, as for me and my household, we shall serve the living God."

He must have known all this while what Rahab did for a living. How it must have hurt him, yet he kept silent.

"For the first time," her father continued. "I want to say the blessings of a father over your life, Rahab. Get on your knees; let me bless you right here and right now in the house of the Lord." Her father began to bless her and her siblings as well.

It was almost time for the revival event to wrap up. An altar call was made for believers to come forward in repentance of their sins and confess Jesus Christ as their Lord and Savior for eternal life. Rahab's entire family came forward.

Kofi and Chidi made their way to Rahab's family. They introduced themselves and began to pray over them, pouring anointing oil over each member of her family while making scriptural declarations of deliverance and salvation. The emotions were very sincere. This was a special moment. Although her father was still blind, they noticed her mother was visibly joyful and engaged in the worship experience. They felt hopeful about their new declaration of faith. They felt seen by the Almighty God Himself.

Apostle Joshua's church in Africa prepared for this very revival mission in a special way. For seven days, the church gathered at midnight to pray and sing praises to God. They also fasted throughout the seven days. In addition, they declared the following scriptures and made prophetic declarations by faith, which is miraculously manifesting at the revival event -

> *But at midnight Paul and Silas were praying and singing hymn to God, and the prisoners were listening to them. Suddenly, there was a great earthquake, so that the foundations of the prison were shaken; and immediately all the doors were opened and everyone's chains were loosed.*
> ***Acts 16: 25, 26 (NKJV).***

> *Therefore, if the son makes you free, you shall be free indeed.*
> ***John 8: 36 (NKJV).***

> *So He [Jesus] said to them, "This kind [of demon] can come out by nothing but prayer and fasting."*
> ***Mark 9: 29 (NKJV).***

CHAPTER 7
Delayed, but Not Denied

It had been exactly 2 weeks since the revival event. Rahab has enrolled in real estate classes online. She went to bed very late from studying and did not plan to wake up so early. Her phone began to ring early in the morning. She saw that it was her brother Jerry. She ignored the call to get some more sleep, but on second thought, she decided to take the call. Before she could accept it, her phone stopped ringing. She called back and he said sharply to her, "you need to come downstairs now."

"Is everything ok?"

"Yes, just come downstairs, please."

She quickly put on a t-shirt over her pajama pants and headed for the elevator to her parents' floor. As soon as she opened the door, she did not need anyone to tell her why she had been called downstairs. Her father's eyes were wide open. He was in tears. He could see.

Rahab could barely contain herself. She began to ask him all sorts of questions to confirm his sight was restored.

"What's the color of my t-shirt?"

"Blue!"

"What's the color of mom's dress?"

"Yellow and Pink!"

"Oh, my goodness!" Rahab shouted. Her mother was on her knees with both hands thrown in the air, praising God. Rahab could not believe the peace and joy that was transforming her family.

Immediately, she called Chidi and shared the good news. Chidi couldn't keep the news to himself. He made a conference call to add Kofi and share the miracle as he broke into a Tim Godfrey and Travis Greene praise song. Kofi joined him to sing along:

"Chukwu n'agwom oria le" [The God Who heals me from sickness]
"When You heal, You heal completely."
"Nara ekele mu oh…" [receive my praises]
"Nara ekele" [receive the praise]
"Nara ekele mu oh…" [receive my praises]
"Nara ekele" [receive the praise]
"Nara ekele mu oh…" [receive my praises]
"What shall I render to Jehovah?"
"For He has done so very much for me…"

"Wow! It has been one testimony after another," Kofi began. "Check out our social media page and see the testimonies. My favorite is a testimony of an American woman whose nonverbal 11-year-old son was delivered from severe autism after the New York Revival. What a joy, Rahab! In the name of Jesus Christ, we declare God's healing grace over the sick among us. Autism, you are defeated in the name of Jesus!

"Amen!" Chorused Chidi and Rahab.

"We declare that the spirit of blindness is forever cast out from the children of God in the name of Jesus Christ."

"Amen!"

"We speak freedom and deliverance from any wicked spirit because who the Son, Jesus sets free is free indeed."

"Amen!"

As they prayed and rejoiced over these testimonies and made more declarations, Rahab put on her earbuds and scrolled straight to their social media page. To her surprise, she found the face of the woman who sat behind her at the Revival on the video testimony post. The 'before' videos captured exactly what she saw at the revival arena, while the 'after' video shows the young boy making eye contact, speaking, and interacting like every other child. He did not wear a helmet. Rahab was shocked to even hear the boy praising God alongside his mom.

Chidi interrupted her over the phone call and asked: "Before I hang up, have you found a church, Rahab?"

"Yes, I prayed for God to lead us to a church, and I found one not too far from us. Our first service as a family will be this weekend. I'm excited but a bit skeptical."

"Why?" He asked.

"It seems like another mega church, and I'm scared they may be running the church as a business and not the house of the Lord."

"Rahab," Chidi began. "Not all mega churches are bad. According to the Bible in the book of Acts chapter two, the Lord adds to the body of Christ daily. False Christians cannot outnumber the true Christians. It's not scriptural. If the Lord has led you to a mega church, trust Him. By the way, what is the name of the church?"

"It's called Victorious Global Church of Christ."

"That sounds familiar. I remember, it was one of the churches that supported our Revival. Their pastor volunteered his premises, but we had already secured the arena. You should be in good hands. Rahab, I hear the Holy Spirit confirming to me that you'll be fine in that church."

"I agree. I felt convinced about the statement of faith posted on their website. But I guess the unpleasant experience from my former church is interfering with what God is doing. Thanks, Chidi. I feel better about this now."

"Awesome. Let me know how it goes, my dear sister in Christ."

"I sure will. Thank you so much."

"I should be thanking you, my dear sister," he said.

"Rahab?"

"Yes," she responded.

"May I ask just one more thing?"

"Sure," she said.

"Now that you have confessed Jesus Christ as your Lord and Savior, the next step according to the Great

Commission given to us in several scriptures including Matthew chapter 28 and Mark, chapter 16 verses 15 and 16 is water baptism. When we come to believe in Jesus Christ, we need to publicly declare our faith in Christ Jesus as our resurrected Savior and Redeemer. Is this something that you feel led to do? If so, are you ready to schedule your water baptism in your new church?"

"Yes, Chidi, I have been reading the daily Bible devotional on the website of your church in Africa. I learned this is an appropriate next step, and I'll be more than glad to pursue water baptism at my new church."

"Great. Let me know if you need anything - a prayer, encouragement, or anything at all. Thanks again and have a blessed day, my dear sister."

"Thanks, and you too, dear." They hung up.

CHAPTER 8
Deliverance and Destruction

The service had just ended when the man who sat beside Rahab introduced himself and asked if she was new. She said "yes."

"Wow! Welcome to our church. My name is Salmon.

"As in Salmon? The fish? Sorry, I didn't mean to be rude." Rahab apologized.

"It's fine," he replied. "I get that reaction all the time. To answer your question, yes, the same way you spell the fish."

"Oh wow! So, tell me, do you get offended when you go out with your friends, and they order salmon?

"Why don't I let you find out for yourself? Dinner tomorrow? How about 6pm?"

"Are you asking me out to dinner? But you barely know me." He was charming, for sure, but Rahab wasn't trying to flirt.

"The more reason we should go out to dinner, so that I can get to know you." He smiled and pulled out his cell phone. "Please enter your name and phone number. I watched you praise the Lord with everything in you and I want to know this woman of God."

Seeing how her worship attracted her to him, she felt comfortable exchanging numbers with Salmon. It was refreshing to get a man's attention not for her body but for the Body of Christ. From risqué to redeemed. What a blessing of deliverance from a risqué lifestyle. All glory to God.

Thankfully, her family sat a few rows in front of her, in a space reserved for the senior citizens; otherwise, she would have been embarrassed to exchange numbers in front of them. This also afforded her a good view of her parents as they worshipped the Lord with gladness.

When Rahab made it back into the seclusion of her apartment, she quickly took a nap and woke up to fix herself a meal. She turned on her TV and began to heat up some food in the microwave when the Breaking News alert flashed on her television. Seeing the caption, she let out a scream and began to cry profusely.

A gunman with mental health issues had attacked Everyone's Light Church during the 11am service, the same service time she attended her former church. Even in her sinful lifestyle, she had attended religiously and would have been there during the attack. Although she didn't learn much about God or His Word in her former church, she was sad to hear the news of an attack.

The news report confirmed the gunman attacked the church with an automatic rifle. When the church security opened fire towards him, the gunman detonated some explosives, which injured more victims. The death toll was still rising, and final count of victims were yet to be confirmed. Many were wounded and hospitalized. Among the victims who were confirmed dead were Mr. Larry Benson and Pastor Derrick Smith. This was the sad fate of her former church.

"Thank you, Jesus! Thank you, God!" "Thank you, Jesus! Thank you, God!" Rahab cried out repeatedly!

THE END.

EPILOGUE

According to the gospel of Matthew on the lineage of Jesus Christ, "Salmon begat Boaz by Rahab (Matthew 1:5). Based on this scripture, Rahab married Salmon and they both gave birth to Boaz."

Although Rahab was encountered in the Bible prior to the birth of Jesus Christ, this historical fiction does reference Jesus Christ as if He had already come. The purpose of doing so is to depict what God asks of any harlot in our modern day - Believe, repent, and be saved.

Any sort of sin against God is a form of harlotry. Therefore, Rahab's character represents any sin that stands in the way of our repentance and salvation that is in Christ Jesus.

> *"For all have sinned and fall short of the glory of God, being justified freely by His grace through the redemption that is in Christ Jesus."*
> **Romans 3: 23, 24 (NKJV).**

The story of Rahab, as told originally in the bible, can be found in the Bible book of Joshua chapters 2 and 6. In the scriptural account, the physical walls of Jericho were brought down during God's war against Jericho. In this fictional version, the spiritual walls of sin that separates us from the Body of Christ were brought down when Rahab and her family confessed Jesus as Lord and Savior. This is a story of *faith*, *repentance*, and *salvation* that is in Christ Jesus.

> *"... if you confess with your mouth the Lord Jesus and believe in your heart that God raised Him from the dead, you will be saved."*
> **Romans 10: 9 (NKJV).**

Rahab: Beyond Risqué

ABOUT THE AUTHOR

Dr. Chioma was born and raised in the West African nation of Nigeria. She received her BA in English from Imo State University in 2003. When she got married in 2005, she relocated to the United States to join her husband. In addition to second bachelor's degree, she earned a master's degree in education from Minot State University, North Dakota.

In 2010, Dr. Chioma moved with her family from North Dakota to Atlanta, Georgia. There, she received a Post master's degree (Ed.S.) in Instructional Technology from Kennesaw State University, Georgia. For her doctorate, she graduated from Valdosta State University with a major in Leadership.

www.doctorchioma.com
Instagram: @doctor.chioma
YouTube: @doctor.chioma

Rahab: Beyond Risqué

Rahab: Beyond Risqué

Rahab: Beyond Risqué

Made in United States
Orlando, FL
08 July 2024